WHAT IS TRUTH?

ANDREW FULLER (1754–1815)

SERIES

WHAT IS

Truth?

ANDREW FULLER

Foreword by Michael A.G. Haykin

H&E
Publishing

IN PARTNERSHIP WITH

Andrew Fuller
CENTER *for* BAPTIST STUDIES
at THE SOUTHERN BAPTIST THEOLOGICAL SEMINARY

What is Truth?

All Scripture quotations are Fuller's own adaptations/partial quotes from the King James Version.

Published by: H&E Publishing, Peterborough, Canada
The Andrew Fuller Center for Baptist Studies is under the auspices of The Southern Baptist Theological Seminary, Louisville, Kentucky

Editors: Chance Faulkner and Corey M.K. Hughes
Cover: Small Meadow Study, 2017 by Melissa Bothwell-Inglis

Source in Public Domain: Andrew Fuller, *Dialogues, Letters, and Essays, on Various Subjects. To Which is Annexed, An Essay on Truth: Containing An Inquiry into its Nature and Importance with The Causes of Error, and The Reasons of its Being Permitted,* 2nd American Edition Published by Samuel Swift, 1811

ISBN 978-1-7752633-5-7
First Edition, 2018
Printed in Canada

CONTENTS

Publishers Note

In this edition, the punctuation and capitalization have been modernized, some archaic words have been updated, and a few other slight editorial changes made.

Acknowledgments

Thank you, Michael Haykin for your help to ensure quality as well as for your encouragement in each of our publications. We also want to thank Benjamin Inglis and Roy Paul for their proofreading this work.

WHO WAS

ANDREW FULLER (1754-1815)?

Michael A. G. Haykin

Andrew Fuller was born in Wicken, a small agricultural village in Cambridgeshire, in 1754.[1] His parents Robert Fuller (1723-1781) and Philippa Gunton (1726-1816), were farmers who rented a succession of dairy farms. In 1761 his parents moved a short distance to Soham, where he and his family began to regularly attend the local Calvinistic Baptist church, and where Fuller was converted in November, 1769. After being baptized the following spring, he became a member of

---

[1] For Fuller's life, the classic study is that of John Ryland, *The Work of Faith, the Labour of Love, and the Patience of Hope Illustrated; in the Life and Death of the Reverend Andrew Fuller* (London: Button & Son, 1816). A second edition of this biography appeared in 1818. For more recent studies, see Arthur H. Kirkby, *Andrew Fuller (1754-1815)* (London: Independent Press Ltd., 1961) and Phil Roberts, "Andrew Fuller" in Timothy George and David S. Dockery, eds., *Baptist Theologians* (Nashville: Broadman Press, 1990), 121-139.

the Soham church. In 1774 Fuller was called to the pastorate of this work. He stayed until 1782, when he became the pastor of the Calvinistic Baptist congregation at Kettering.

His time as a pastor in Soham was a decisive period for the shaping of Fuller's theological perspective. It was during this period that he began a life-long study of the works of the American divine Jonathan Edwards (1703–1758), which, along with his commitment to live under the authority of the infallible Scriptures, enabled him to become what his close friend John Ryland, Jr. (1753–1825) described as "perhaps the most judicious and able theological writer that ever belonged to our denomination."[2] Succeeding generations have confirmed Ryland's estimation of his friend. The Victorian Baptist preacher, C.H. Spurgeon (1834–1892), for instance, once described Fuller as the "greatest theologian" of his century, while A.C. Underwood, the Baptist historian of this century, said of Fuller—in a statement that clearly echoes Ryland's estimation—that "he was the soundest and most creatively useful theologian the Particular Baptists have ever had."[3]

The text reproduced in the following pages is typical of the reasoning powers of Fuller. It first appeared as a preface

---

[2] *The Indwelling and Righteousness of Christ no Security against Corporeal Death, but the Source of Spiritual and Eternal Life* (London, 1815), 2–3.

[3] The Spurgeon remark is taken from Gilbert Laws, *Andrew Fuller: Pastor, Theologian, Ropeholder* (London: Carey Press, 1942), 127; A. C. Underwood, *A History of the English Baptists* (London: The Baptist Union Publication Dept. [Kingsgate Press], 1947), 166.

of sorts to Hannah Adams, A View of Religions (British edition, 1805) and was entitled "An Essay on Truth."[4] Typical of eighteenth-century thinkers, both Christian and non-Christian, Fuller believed that there was such a thing as truth, and that it could be known. His essay is thus a primer of what he calls "evangelical truth."[5] Here he lays out, with copious biblical support, what is the truth about the present state of humanity, that is, their fallenness, and the sole remedy for that state, namely, faith in the crucified and risen Christ as Lord. While his topic, "What is truth?," might be conceived primarily as a philosophical question, he tackles it biblically and shows the way in which this conviction about Christ permeated the thinking of the early church. He also delineates its importance and how true virtue must proceed from it—here he is responding to the claims of various eighteenth-century moralists who thought they could be good without faith in the God of the Bible. Moreover, if there is truth, then there must also be error. Fuller thus discusses what are the various roots of error and why it exists.

While these are difficult matters for modern men and women to discuss and even conceive—to many moderns, such a discussion about truth and error smacks of triumphalism—Fuller's historical context, the long eighteenth century, enabled him to set forth his conviction

---

[4] Andrew Fuller, "An Essay on Truth" in Hannah Adams, *A View of Religions, in Three Parts* (New ed.; London: W. Button & Son/T. Williams & Co., 1805), 5–30.

[5] See below, page 6.

that truth does indeed exist, and that our eternal destiny hangs upon discovering it and avoiding error of the first degree. For the so-called post-modern West, a text like this is oh-so-needed! It deflates the pride of western thought, which uses the concept of diversity to masquerade as humility, and reasserts a central element of God's revelation, the saving work of Jesus Christ as humanity's only hope. Indeed, it is the embrace of this that produces the sweetness of true humility.

Michael A. G. Haykin, FRHistS
Professor of Church History & Biblical Spirituality,
Director of The Andrew Fuller Center for Baptist Studies,
The Southern Baptist Theological Seminary, Louisville, Kentucky.

INTRODUCTION

The multifarious and discordant sentiments which divide mankind afford a great temptation to skepticism, and many are carried away by it. The open enemies of the gospel take occasion from such to justify their rejection of it and many of its professed friends have written as if they thought that to be decided, amidst so many minds and opinions, would be almost presumptuous. The principal, if not the only use which they would make of these differences, is to induce a spirit of moderation and charity, and to declaim against bigotry.

To say nothing at present how these terms are perverted and hackneyed in a certain cause, let two things be seriously considered. First, whether this was the use made by the apostles of the discordant opinions which prevailed in their times, even amongst those who acknowledged the divinity of our Saviour's mission? In differences amongst Christians which did not affect the kingdom of God, nor destroy the work of God, it certainly was. Such were those concerning meats, drinks, and days,[6] in which the utmost forbearance was inculcated. But it was otherwise in differences which affected the leading doctrines and precepts of Christianity. Forbearance in these cases would, in the account of the sacred writers, have been a crime.

Let us candidly inquire, Christian reader, notwithstanding the diversity of sentiments in the Christian world: 1. Whether truth may not be clearly ascertained. 2. Whether it be not of the utmost importance. 3. Whether the prevalence of error may not be accounted for. 4. Lastly, whether the wisdom, as well as the justice of God, may not be seen in his permitting it.

---

[6] Romans 14:17, 20.

1

WHAT IS TRUTH?

In attempting to answer this question, I desire to take nothing for granted but that Christianity is of God, and that the Scriptures are a revelation of his will. If Christianity be of God, and he has revealed his will in the holy Scriptures, light is come into the world, though the dark minds of sinful creatures comprehend it not. It does not follow that because many wander in mazes of fruitless speculation, that there is not a way so plain that a wayfaring man, or one who "walks in the truth,"[7] though a fool, shall not err. The numerous sects among the Greeks, Romans, and even among the Jews, at the time of our Saviour's appearing, did not prove that there was no certain knowledge to be obtained of what was truth. Our Lord considered himself as speaking plainly, or he would not

---

[7] 3 John 1:4.

have asked the Jews as he did, "Why do you not understand my speech?"[8] The apostles and primitive believers saw their way plainly and, though we cannot pretend to the extraordinary inspiration which was possessed by many of them yet if we humbly follow their light, depending on the ordinary teachings of God's Holy Spirit, we shall see ours.

Truth, we may be certain, is the same thing as what in the Scriptures is denominated, "the gospel," "the common salvation," "the common faith," "the faith once delivered to the saints," "the truth as it is in Jesus," etc. and what this is may be clearly understood by the brief summaries of the gospel, and of the faith of the primitive Christians which abound in the New Testament. Of the former the following are a few of many examples:

> God so loved the world that he gave his only begotten Son, that whosoever believes in him should not perish, but have everlasting life (John 3:16).

> The Son of Man came to seek and save that which is lost (Matt. 18:11).

> I am the way, the truth, and the life; no man comes to the Father but by me (John 14:6).

> To him give all the prophets witness, that through his name whosoever believes in him shall receive remission of sins (Acts 10:43).

---

[8] John 8:43.

We preach Christ crucified, to the Jews a stumbling-block, and to the Greeks foolishness; but to them that believe, the wisdom of God, and the power of God (1 Cor. 1:23).

I determined not to know anything among you, save Jesus Christ, and him crucified (1 Cor. 2:2).

Moreover, brethren, I declare to you the gospel which I preached to you, which also you have received, and wherein you stand; by which also you are saved, if you hold fast what I preached to you, unless you have believed in vain; for I delivered to you first of all, that which I also received, how that Christ died for our sins, according to the Scriptures; and that he was buried, and that he rose again the third day according to the Scriptures (1 Cor. 15:1–4).

This is a faithful saying, and worthy of all acceptation, that Christ came into the world to save sinners, of whom I am chief (1 Tim. 1:15).

This is the record, that God has given to us eternal life, and this life is in his Son (1 Jn. 5:11).

Neither is there salvation in any other: for there is none other name under heaven given among men, whereby we must be saved (Acts 4:12).

If language have any determinate meaning, it is here plainly taught that mankind are not only sinners, but in a lost and perishing condition, without help or hope, but what arises from the free grace of God, through the atonement of his Son. That he died as our substitute. That we are forgiven and accepted only for the sake of what he has done and suffered. That in his person and work all evangelical truth concentrates. That the doctrine of salvation for the chief of sinners through his death was so familiar in the primitive times as to become a kind of Christian proverb and that on our receiving and retaining this depends our present standing, and final salvation. If this doctrine be received, Christianity is received. If not, the record which God has given of his Son is rejected, and he himself treated as a liar.

When this doctrine is received in the true spirit of it, which it never is but by a sinner ready to perish, all those fruitless speculations, which tend only to bewilder the mind, will be laid aside; just as malice, guile, envies, and evil-speakings, are laid aside by him who is born of God.[9] They will fall off from the mind of their own accord, like the coat of the chrysalis. Many instances of this are constantly occurring. Persons who, after having read and studied controversies, and leaned first to one opinion and then to another, till their minds have been lost in uncertainty, have at length been brought to think of the gospel, not as a matter of speculation, but as that which seriously and immediately concerned them. Having embraced it as good news to them who are ready to perish, they have found not only rest to their souls, but that

---

[9] 1 Peter 2:1.

all their former notions have departed from them, as a dream when one awakes.

Corresponding with the brief summaries of the gospel are the concise accounts given of the faith of the primitive Christians:

Whosoever believes that Jesus is the Christ, is born of God... (1 Jn. 5:1).

Who is he that overcomes the world, but he that believes that Jesus is the Son of God? (1 Jn. 5:5).

If you shall confess with your mouth the Lord Jesus, and believe in your heart that God has raised him from the dead, you shall be saved (Rom. 10:9).

The sacred writers did not mean, by this language, to magnify the belief of one or two divine truths at the expense of others, but to exhibit them as bearing an inseparable connection. This is so that, if these were truly embraced, the others would be certain to accompany them. They considered the doctrine of the person and work of Christ as a golden link that would draw along with it the whole chain of evangelical truth. Hence, we perceive the propriety of such language as the following:

He that has the Son, has life; and he that has not the Son, has not life—Whosoever denies the Son, the same has not the Father..." (1 Jn. 5:12; 2:23).

The doctrine and the faith of the primitive Christians were summarily avowed every time they celebrated the Lord's Supper. The leading truth exhibited by that ordinance is the same which John calls "the record," namely that, "God has given to us eternal life, and this life is in his Son."[10] Under the form of a feast, of which we are invited to take, eat, and drink, we see the blessings of the New Testament; the medium through which they were obtained, namely, "the blood of Jesus, shed for many, for the remission of sins;"[11] and the way in which they must be received; that is to say, as a free gift, bestowed on the unworthy for his sake. If this simple doctrine were believed with the spirit of a little child, and lived upon as our meat and drink, we might take an everlasting leave of speculations on things beyond our reach without sustaining the loss of anything but what were better lost than retained.

---

[10] 1 John 5:11.
[11] Matthew 26:28.

2

IMPORTANCE OF TRUTH

If the above remarks may be thought sufficient to ascertain what is truth, its importance follows as a necessary consequence. If, as transgressors, we be exposed to the eternal displeasure of our Maker; if a door of hope be opened to us; if it be at no less an expense than the death of God's only begotten Son in our nature; and if, through this great propitiation, God can be just and the justifier of believers; and if this be the only way of escape, and the present the only state in which it is possible to flee to it for refuge, who that is not infatuated by the delusions of this world, can make light of it?

There is an importance in truth as it is found in philosophy, history, politics, or any other branch of science that affects the present happiness of mankind; but what is this when compared with that which involves their everlasting salvation? To be furnished with an answer to the question, "What shall I do to be saved"[12] is of infinitely greater account than to be able to decide whether the Ptolemaic or Copernican system be that of nature. The temporal salvation of a nation, great as it is and greatly as it interests the minds of men, is nothing when compared with the eternal salvation of a single individual.

But many who would not deny the superior value of eternal salvation to all other things, have yet gone about to depreciate the importance of divine truth, and to represent it as having no necessary connection with either present holiness or future happiness. Such appears to have been the design of those well-known line of Pope:

> For modes of faith let graceless zealots fight:
> His can't be wrong whose life is in the right.[13]

And to the same purpose we have often been told in prose, that, "we shall not be judged at the last day by our opinions, but by our works."[14] If truth and error existed in the mind merely as opinions or objects of speculation, they might possibly have but little influence upon us; but if they be principles of action, they enter into the essence of all we do. Such is the influence of living faith, otherwise it could not be shown by our works. Such is that of the belief of falsehood,

---

[12] Acts 16:30.
[13] Alexander Pope, *An Essay on Man*, Epistle III, lines 305–306.
[14] 2 Corinthians 5:10; Romans 2:6.

else we had not read of the word of false teachers, "eating as does a canker."[15] The works by which we shall be judged cannot mean actions in distinction from their principles; for as such they would contain neither good nor evil, but only as connected with them. All pretences therefore, to separate the one from the other, are as contrary to reason as they are to Scripture.

To render this subject more evident, let the following particulars be duly considered.

It is by the belief of truth that sinners are brought into a state of salvation

Great things are ascribed in the Scriptures to faith, but faith could have no existence without revealed truth as its foundation. Whatever importance, therefore, attaches to the one attaches to the other. The great blessing of justification is constantly ascribed to faith—not as the reward of a virtue, but as that by which we become one with Christ, and so partakers of his benefits. While unbelievers, we have no revealed interest in the divine favour, but are declared to be under condemnation. Believing in him, we are no longer, "under the law," as a term of life and death, but, "under grace."[16] Hence it is that in the gospel, as "heard and received," we are said to "stand."[17] Take away evangelical truth, and you take away the standing of a Christian.

---

[15] James 2:18; 2 Timothy 2:17.
[16] Romans 6:14.
[17] Ephesians 1:13; 2 Timothy 3:14; Colossians 1:23.

Bereaved of this, the best man upon earth must despair of salvation.

Truth is the model and standard of true religion in the mind

Doctrines, whether true or false, if really believed, become principles of action. That they are a mould into which the mind is cast, and from which it receives its impression, is evident both from Scripture and experience. An observant eye will easily perceive a spirit which attaches to different species of religion; and which, over and above the diversities arising from natural temper, will manifest itself in their respective followers. Paganism, Mahometanism,[18] Deism, Apostate Judaism, and various systems which have appeared under the name of Christianity, have each discovered a spirit of their own. Thus also it was from the beginning. Those who received "another doctrine," received with it "another spirit," and hence we read of, "the spirit of truth, and the spirit of error."[19] He that had the one is said to be "of God," and he that had the other, "not of God."[20]

Revealed truth is represented as a form of doctrine into which believers are delivered.[21] As a melted substance, cast into a mould, receives its form from it, and every line in the one corresponds with that of the other; so true religion in the

---

[18] *Mohometanism* meaning Islam, the faith of Muslims.
[19] 1 John 4:1–6.
[20] 2 Corinthians 11:4; 1 John 4:6.
[21] Romans 6:17.

soul accords with true religion in the Scriptures. Without this standard we shall either model our faith by our own preconceived notions of what is fit and reasonable, or be carried away by our feelings, and lose ourselves among the extravagant vagaries of enthusiasm. Our views may seem to us very rational, or our feelings may be singularly ardent, and yet we may be far from being in the right. The question is whether they agree, line to line, with the divine model?

God says in his Word, "Seek my face."[22] If our hearts say to him, "Your face Lord, I will seek," then does line answer to line, and this is true religion. Is it a leading feature of evangelical truth, that it honours the divine character and government? It is the same with true religion in the mind. Does that manifest love even to enemies? So does this. Is it the object of the former to abase the pride of man? It is no less the nature of the latter to rejoice in lying low. Finally, is the one averse to all iniquity, and friendly to universal holiness? The other, dissatisfied with present attainment, presses towards the mark for the prize of the high calling of God in Christ Jesus.[23]

Truth is that which furnishes the motive for every exercise of true holiness
If once we are enabled to behold its glory, the glory of God in the face of Jesus Christ, it changes us into the same image, begets and excites holy affections, and every kind of gracious

---

[22] Psalm 27:8.
[23] Philippians 3:14.

exercise. Hence we are said to, "know the truth, and the truth to make us free." To be "sanctified" through it, and "begotten" by it.[24]

It is not denied that there is much of what is called morality in persons who know and believe nothing to purpose of evangelical truth. Honour, interest, and the habits of education, will induce men to shun open immoralities, and to comply with things which are reputable and praiseworthy. But though there be great cause for thankfulness to God who, by his providence, thus restrains mankind from much evil, yet this is not holiness. Holiness is the love of God and one another, whereas this is mere self-love. All works and worship of this kind are no better than the offering of Cain which, being without faith, could not please God.

And as there may be a semblance of holiness without faith, so there may be a semblance of faith without holiness. The doctrines of the Bible, though in themselves practical, yet may be treated as mere speculations, and frequently are so by men who profess to believe them. Where this is the case, instead of producing holiness, they may have a contrary effect—but this is owing to their being perverted. God's words do good to the upright. There is not a sentiment in the living oracles but what, if received in the true spirit and intent of it, will contribute to the sanctification of the mind.

---

[24] John 8:32; 17:17; James 1:18.

True religion is, with great beauty and propriety called, "Walking in the truth."[25] A life of sobriety, righteousness, and godliness, is Christian principle reduced to practice. Truth is a system of love, an overflow of the divine blessedness, as is intimated by its being called, "The glorious gospel of the blessed God."[26] It is a system of reconciliation, peace, and forgiveness, full of the most amazing condescension and spotless rectitude. To walk in truth like this is to walk in love. To be tenderhearted, forgiving one another, even as God for Christ's sake has forgiven us.[27] To be of the same mind with him who made himself of no reputation, and took upon him the form of a servant, and to be holy in all manner of conversation.

Such were the fruits of truth which were actually brought forth by the primitive believers. Such different degrees, notwithstanding the many defects and scandals which abound amongst us, are the fruits of it in true Christians to this day. Thousands of examples, both in earlier and later times, might be produced in which men who previously walked according to the course of this world,[28] in rioting and drunkenness, in chambering[29] and wantonness, in strife and envying,[30] on embracing the doctrine of Christ crucified, have put off all these, and become new creatures.

---

[25] 3 John 4.
[26] 1 Timothy 1:11.
[27] Ephesians 4:32.
[28] Ephesians 2:2.
[29] *Chambering* meaning illicit intercourse; sexual immorality.
[30] Romans 13:13.

It is also worthy of special notice that in every instance in which the primitive churches deviated from the doctrine of the apostles, they appear to have degenerated in zeal and practical godliness. A careful review of the epistles to the Corinthians, Galatians, and Hebrews, who departed more than any other churches from the simplicity of the gospel, would furnish proof of the justness of this remark. It was not without reason that Paul observed to the Corinthians, "Evil communications corrupt good manners,"[31] by which he appears to have meant the communications of false teachers, who endeavoured to undermine the resurrection, and other important truths. And such was the "corruption of manners" which accompanied these notions, that, degenerate as we consider ourselves compared with the primitive Christians, if any one of our churches tolerated the same things, we should be almost ready to pronounce it a synagogue of Satan. Among other things, they divided into parties, boasted of the talents of their preachers, connived[32] at the most unnatural kind of fornication, went to law with one another, communed with idolaters at their temples, and profaned the supper of the Lord, by appropriating it to purposes of sensual indulgence! Such were the fruits of error.

If we look into the epistle to the Galatians, who had been turned aside from the apostolic doctrine of justification, we shall find fruits of the same kind. They are described as "not

---

[31] 1 Corinthians 15:33.
[32] *Connived* meaning secretly allow something.

obeying the truth," as "foolish," as in a manner "bewitched," as having lost their former "zeal," and rendered their Christianity a matter of "doubt," as needing to have "Christ again formed in them," and it is strongly intimated that they were guilty of "biting," and "devouring" one another. They were, "fulfilling the lusts of the flesh," and, "of coveting vain glory, provoking one another, and envying one another."[33]

If the Hebrews had not, in turning aside from the truth, been injured in their spirit and conduct, it is very improbable that such language as the following would have been addressed to them:

> Therefore, as the Holy Spirit says, "Today, if you will hear his voice, harden not your hearts, as in the provocation, in the day of temptation in the wilderness, when your fathers tempted me, proved me, and saw my works forty years. Therefore, I was grieved with that generation, and said, "They do always err in their hearts and they have not known my ways. So I swore in my wrath, they shall not enter into my rest."—Take heed, brethren, lest there be in any of you an evil heart of unbelief, in departing from the living God? Exhort one another daily while it is called today, lest any of you be hardened through the deceitfulness of sin (Heb. 3:7–13).

---

[33] See Galatians 3:1; 4:11, 19, 20; 5:7, 15, 26.

Neither is it likely that they would have been exhorted to the following, if no such symptoms had appeared amongst them:

Look diligently, lest any man should fail of the grace of God; lest any root of bitterness springing up should trouble them, and thereby many be defiled; lest there should be any fornicator, or profane person, as Esau, who for one morsel of meat sold his birthright (Heb. 12:15–16).

Finally, it is not probable that so solemn a warning against "whoredom and adultery" would have been introduced, and the offenders cited to the tribunal of God, if there has been no occasion for their own conduct.

Whether these instances of the pernicious efforts of error in the primitive churches be not in direct opposition to the modern notions before stated, let the reader judge. Nor are such things peculiar to the primitive churches. If you see men desert the principles before stated, or hold them in a corrupted sense, you may commonly perceive a change in their spirit.

They may retain what is called character, in the eyes of the world, but the savour of godliness is departed. They may retain their zeal, but it will be confined to some little peculiarity, to the neglect of the common faith. There will be a want of that lovely proportion which constitutes the true beauty of holiness. A man who chews opium, or tobacco, may prefer them to the most wholesome food, and may derive from them pleasure, and even vigour for a time; but his pale countenance, and debilitated constitution, will soon bear witness to the folly of spending his money for that which is not bread.

The love which the primitive Christians bore to one another was for the truth's sake[34]

Now the reason for which we love a person is considered as of greater importance than anything else pertaining to him. It is that which constitutes his value in our esteem and which, if he abandon, we should no longer esteem him.

Here we may perceive what is essential to the true, legitimate charity of the primitive Christians. Instead of regarding men irrespectively of their principles, they "knew no man after the flesh."[35] John, who was the most loving, or charitable of all the disciples of Christ, is so far from considering a departure from the truth as a light matter, and the subject of it as entitled to the same Christian affection as heretofore, that he expressly writes as follows:

> Whosoever transgresses, and abides not in *the doctrine of Christ*, has not God. If there come any to you, and bring not this doctrine, receive *him not into your house*, neither bid him God speed; for he that bids him Godspeed, is *partaker of his evil deeds* (2 Jn. 9–11, emphasis added).

---

[34] 2 John 2; 3 John 1.
[35] 2 Corinthians 5:16.

Would not such language, I ask, in our days be reckoned very uncharitable? It would. But this proves beyond all reasonable doubt that the common ideas of charity are anti-scriptural. Charity will not take it for granted that whosoever deviates from our views must needs deviate from the doctrine of Christ, but will carefully inquire at the oracles of God what is truth. Yet there is no need of being ever learning, and never able to come to the knowledge of it. The lady whom John addressed was supposed to be able to distinguish between those who "brought the doctrine of Christ," and those who came without it; and so are Christians in the present day.[36] Charity "hopes all things,"[37] and will always put the most favourable construction upon the motives of others that truth will admit, but without truth as its ground and guide, it will not proceed.

Here also we may see the nature of Christian unity. It is not merely for two or more persons to be agreed; for this they may be in evil. This is mere party attachment. It is natural for men to love those who think and act like themselves, and that for their own sake. But Christian unity is to love one another for Christ's sake, and for the truth's sake that dwells in them. Christ, as revealed in the gospel, forms the great point of union. A number of minds are drawn towards this point and the nearer they approximate to it, the nearer they approach to a union with one another. If all true Christians were nearer to

---

[36] 2 John.
[37] 1 Corinthians 13:7.

the mind of Christ, their differences would soon subside and they would feel themselves, as they approached it, to be of one heart and soul.

Truth is the only solid foundation of peace and happiness

There are cases it is granted, in which the mind may rejoice in error, and be distressed by truth. False doctrine will operate like opium, thrilling the imagination with pleasing dreams—but all is transient and delusive. Truth on the other hand, when it barely commends itself to the conscience of a sinner, may render him extremely unhappy. Such was the effect of Judas's conviction of Christ's innocence,[38] and such is the effect of similar convictions in the present times. But where truth takes possession of the heart, or, as the Scriptures express it, where we "receive the love of the truth,"[39] peace and joy accompany it. This is a fact established by history and experience, and is easily accounted for.

Revealed truth carries in it a message of pardon, reconciliation, and eternal life, and all in a way honourable to the divine character and government. This, in itself, is good news, and to everyone who, as a sinner ready to perish, receive it, is a source of solid and lasting happiness. Truth also pours light upon all the dark and mysterious events of time and teaches us, while weeping over human misery, not to despond or repine but, viewing things on a large scale, to

---

[38] Matthew 27:3.
[39] 2 Thessalonians 2:10.

rejoice in whatever is. It exhibits God upon the throne of the universe, ordering everything for the best; and thus reconciles the mind to present ill, by pointing it to the good that shall ultimately rise out of it.

Contrast with this the horrible complaints of an infidel:

Who can, without horror, consider the whole earth as the empire of destruction? It abounds in wonders; it abounds also in victims; it is a vast field of carnage and contagion! Every species is without pity; pursued and torn to pieces, through the earth, and air, and water! In man there is more wretchedness than in all other animals put together. He smarts continually under two scourges, which other animals never feel; anxiety and listlessness in appetence, which make him weary of himself. He loves life, and yet he knows that he must die. If he enjoy some transient; good, for which he is thankful to Heaven, he suffers various evils, and is at last devoured by worms. This knowledge is his fatal prerogative. Other animals have it not. He feels it every moment rankling and corroding in his breast. Yet he spends the transient moment of his existence in diffusing the misery which he suffers; in cutting the throats of his fellow creatures for pay; in cheating, and being cheated; in robbing and being robbed; in serving, that he may command; and in repenting of all that he does. The bulk of mankind are nothing more than a crowd of wretches, equally criminal and unfortunate; and the globe contains rather carcasses than men. I tremble upon a review of this dreadful picture, to find that it implies a complaint against Providence; and I wish that I had never been born.[40]

Such is the boasted happiness of unbelievers! And though we should not go these lengths yet, if we forsake truth, by deviating materially from any of the great doctrines of the gospel, it will affect our peace. Error is the wandering of a tired mind when it thinks without a guide, the result of which is, "stumbling upon the dark mountains."[41] It is possible, in such circumstances, that the stupor of insensibility may be mistaken for the peace of God; but if the soul be once roused from its slumber, especially if it be the subject of any true religion, it will find itself miserable. As soon we might expect to find happiness in the mind of one who has lost his way, and knows not wither he goes, as in a mind that has deviated from evangelical truth.

---

[40] Voltaire as cited in David Simpson, *A Plea for Religion, and the Sacred Writings, Addressed to the Disciples of Thomas Paine, and wavering Christians of every Persuasion* (2nd ed.; London: T. Conder, 1803), p.180, n.*.

[41] Jeremiah 13:16.

3

CAUSES OF ERROR

If truth be of this importance, it may be inquired how we are to account for the great diversity of sentiment in the religious world? Whence is it that professing Christians, even the wise and the good amongst them, should be so divided?

It certainly is not owing to anything in Christianity itself. This will be found, on the strictest inquiry, to be one consistent whole, and all its precepts tend to unity of judgment, as well as of affection. To this end were all the epistles addressed to the primitive churches. In some, the writers labour to establish them in the truth; and others, to reclaim them from error. In all, to promote a holy unanimity in principle and practice.

Yet if we look to fact, we find that the churches, even in the purest ages, were never free from error. It was beyond the power of the apostles, inspired as they were, effectually to guard them against it. Of this, the aforementioned epistles to the Corinthians, Galatians, and the Hebrews, are standing proofs. And in after ages things were much worse. Those principles which at first were but the bud, or at most the blade, now became the full ear, and produced a harvest of corruption and apostasy. The history of Christianity from that day to this is the history of one continued struggle between truth and error; the mind of Christ, and the reasonings of the flesh. Nor was this state of things unknown to the apostles. They saw the mystery of iniquity begin to work in their times, and by the spirit of inspiration foretold its progress:

In the latter times, some shall depart from the faith, giving heed to seducing spirits, and doctrines of demons—In the last days perilous times shall come, in which men shall be lovers of their own selves, ever learning, and never able to come to the knowledge of the truth (1 Tim. 4:1; 2 Tim. 3:1–2, 7).

And that:

As there were false prophets among the [Jewish] people, so there should be false teachers among [Christians,] who would bring in damnable heresies, even denying the Lord that bought them; and bring upon themselves swift destruction (2 Pt. 2:1).

What shall we say then? Shall we attribute the multifarious and discordant doctrines of past and present times to diversity of habits, educations, and connections? To the various tastes and talents found amongst men? Or to the frailty and imbecility of the human mind. These things may be allowed to have their influence, but it is not to them principally that the Scriptures attribute the corruption of Christian doctrine or worship.

There is an important difference between diversity and contrariety. The former belongs to men as men, which the latter does not. One man comprehends more of truth, another less. This man has a talent for discovering one part of truth, and that another. In all this there is nothing more than in a diversity of features, or in the variegated face of the earth, which abounds in diverse kinds of flowers, every one of which contributes to the beauty of the whole. It is not so with respect to truth and error, which are as opposite as right and wrong. True doctrines are the plants, and false doctrines the weeds of the church. They cannot both flourish in the same mind. The one must be rooted up, or the other will be overrun, and rendered unproductive.

The causes which the Scriptures assign for the corruption of Christian doctrine are principally, if not entirely, of a moral nature. They represent evangelical truth as a holy doctrine, and as that which cannot be understood by an unholy mind:

The natural, (or merely worldly-wise,) man, receives not the things of the Spirit of God; for they are foolishness to him: neither can he know them, because they are spiritually discerned (1 Cor. 2:14).

They are, "hid from the wise and prudent, and revealed to babes," and thus, "it seems good in his sight," whose mind it is to abase the pride of man.[42] If the gospel had been the wisdom of this world, then the spirit of this world would have sufficed to understand it, and there would be no more errors concerning it than what arise from the imbecility of the human mind on all other subjects. But it is not. It is the wisdom that is above and, therefore, requires a state of mind suited to it or, as the apostle expresses it, that, "we receive not the spirit of the world, but the spirit which is of God, that we may know the things which are freely given to us of God."[43] Now this being the case, so far as we attempt to judge, preach, or write of the gospel under the influence of mere worldly wisdom, or in any other than its own spirit, we are morally certain in some way or another to pervert it.

Here then are opened to our view three grand sources of error namely: 1. The numbers of unconverted, or merely wordly wise characters who intrude themselves or are intruded by others into the Christian ministry. 2. The greater number of merely nominal Christians, whose taste calls for

---

[42] Matthew 21:25–26.
[43] 1 Corinthians 2:12.

anti-scriptural preaching. 3. The large portion of unsanctified wisdom found even in godly men.

The great number of unconverted ministers

Far be it from me to judge of men otherwise than by what they manifest themselves to be. I abhor the spirit of our modern antinomians, who would persuade us that they know good ministers from others by a kind of spiritual physiognomy.[44] Who, if the tree be known by the fruits, have much more reason to judge themselves. Yet the personal religion of many preachers must be allowed by charity itself to wear more than a suspicious appearance. Nor is it surprising that it should be so. If in the purest age of the church when there were but few attractions for covetousness and ambition, there were "men of corrupt minds, reprobate concerning the faith."[45] There were also men who had, "the form of godliness, but denied the power thereof."[46] Is it any wonder that there should be such in our times? And as the introduction of almost every error amongst the primitive Christians is attributed to this sort of character, it is reasonable to expect that things should still move on in the same direction.

An unrenewed person, whatever be his education, talents, or natural temper, can never fall in with Christianity as it is taught in the New Testament. If, therefore, he occupy a

---

[44] The supposed art of judging character from facial characteristics.
[45] 2 Timothy 3:8.
[46] 2 Timothy 3:5.

station in the church, he will be almost certain to transform religion so as to suit himself. This, it is clear, was the grand source of the Romish apostasy. No sooner was Christianity adopted by the state, than it became the interest of worldly men to profess it. Ecclesiastical offices were soon filled, in a great degree, by unbelievers in disguise. The effect was, as might have been expected, the doctrine, worship, discipline, and spirit of the gospel, were gradually lost and a system of corruption substituted its place.

This has been a source of departure from the truth down to the present time and that, in different degrees, amongst all denominations of Christians. If we look in to the establishments of Protestant Europe we shall find that, in spite of oaths and subscriptions devised in former ages for the security of orthodoxy, worldly men have a system of their own, and will explain their articles and creeds according to it. Or if we look out of establishments, wherever worldly men are admitted to the work of the ministry, we shall find things much the same. Some of the greatest perverters of the gospel during the last century have descended from pious parents, who, fond of the idea of bringing up their children to the public service of God, overlooked the necessity of personal religion; presuming, as it would seem, that God would in due time supply that defect. The consequence was the young men, finding evangelical truth sit uneasily upon them, threw it off, and embraced a system more suited to the state of their minds.

Observing these things among men of education, many serious people have contracted a prejudice against learning itself, and have preferred the preaching of the most illiterate for the sake of a pure doctrine. But neither is this any security since men of assurance and address, pretending to extraordinary light and marvellous inspirations, will often obtrude[47] themselves upon the people and draw disciples after them—especially from amongst the unthinking and light-minded part of Christian professors. In them have the words of Peter been eminently fulfilled:

Speaking great swelling words of vanity, they have allured through the lusts of the flesh, those that for a while were escaped from them who live in error (2 Pt. 2:18).

Nor has their influence been confined to such characters, sincere people have also frequently been misled by their specious pretences. When Judas, professing a solicitude for the poor, condemned an expression of love to Christ as an unnecessary piece of wastefulness, he drew away the other disciples after him. In short, men who have not the spirit by which the gospel was dictated, will not cleave to it. Some may err on this side, and some on that. Some, having greater talents, may do greater injury to it, and others less; but all, in one way or another, will pervert it. Where this is the case,

---

[47] *Obtrude* meaning to impose or force.

"many will follow their pernicious ways; and the way of truth,"[48] being confounded with them, "will be evil spoken of."[49]

The great number of merely nominal Christians

In the present state of things, the bulk of mankind are not governed by principle, but by custom; following the course of this world, whatever direction it may take. In one country they are Heathens, in another, Mahometans,[50] and in another, Christians—in other words, they are of no religion. The effect of this is, that a large proportion of ministers are certain to be nominated and chosen by men who have no taste for the searching, humbling, and holy doctrine of the gospel, but are utterly averse from it. Where this is the case, it requires but little discernment to perceive what will be the general tone of preaching. Even in congregational churches, if the people, or the leading individuals amongst them, be worldly-minded, ambitious, or in any respect loose lives, they will not be at a loss to find preachers after their own heart. Thus error is propagated, and thus it was propagated from a very early period.

> The time will come, when they will not endure sound doctrine; but after their own lusts shall they heap to themselves teachers, having itching ears;

---

[48] 2 Peter 2:2.

[49] Romans 14:16.

[50] *Mohomentans* meaning Muslims.

and they shall turn away their ears from the truth,
and shall be turned to fables (2 Tim. 4:3–4).

The large portion of unsanctified wisdom found even in godly men

The wisdom of this world, as opposed to the wisdom of God, is not confined to mere worldly men. The apostle, after speaking of spiritual men as "judging all things," and as "having the mind of Christ," adds, "And I, brethren, could not speak unto you as unto spiritual, but as to carnal; even as to babes in Christ."[51] And this, their carnality, is represented as rendering them unable to understand the great doctrines of Christianity, which are compared to meat and as leading them to build upon the gospel foundation a mixture of "wood and hay, and stubble," all which shall be burnt up another day, though they themselves shall be saved.[52]

There is a slowness of heart, even in good men, to believe what God has revealed, especially if it clash with their preconceived ideas. Such was the state of mind of the apostles themselves previous to the resurrection of their Lord, and such is the state of mind of great numbers amongst us. We often hear men in controversy talk of being open to conviction and willing to retract their sentiments if but fairly confuted, but such professions either mean but little, or at best indicate a great want of self-knowledge. Those who are the most open to conviction will commonly suspect

[51] 1 Corinthians 3:1.
[52] 1 Corinthians 2:6, 7, 12, 15, 16; 3:1, 2, 12–17.

themselves the most, and will not be very forward in the use of such language. If there were not a slowness of heart, both in receiving truth, and relinquishing error, a large proportion of our controversies would soon be at an end.

4

REASONS WHY ERROR IS PERMITTED

The foregoing remarks may suffice to account for the prevalence of error so far as man is concerned; but it may be further inquired, wherefore does God permit it? Why is it that the beauty of the Christian church is suffered to be marred, and its peace invaded by a succession of perpetual discords? This is an awful subject and, if left to our own conjectures upon it, would be our wisdom to leave it to the great day when all things will be made manifest. But we are not! The Scriptures of truth inform us that, "there must need be heresies, that they who are approved may be made manifest."[53]

All the influences to which we are exposed in the present life are adapted to a state of probation, and do us good or harm according to the state of mind which we possess. We

---

[53] 1 Corinthians 11:19.

are not only "fearfully made,"[54] but as fearfully situated. The evidence in favour of true religion is sufficient for a candid mind, but not for one that is disposed to cavil.[55] If we attend to it simply to find out truth and obey it, we shall not be disappointed; but if our souls be lifted up within us, the very rock of salvation will be to us a stone of stumbling. The Jews require a sign in their own way: "Let him come down from the cross, and we will believe him."[56]

If he had publicly risen from the dead, say modern unbelievers, none could have doubted it, yet he neither came down from the cross, nor rose publicly from the dead. He could not, they continue, and all his miracles were the work of imposture.

It may be our duty, as much as in us lies, to cut off occasion from them who desire such occasion to speak—but God often acts otherwise. They who desire a handle to renounce the gospel, shall have it. Thus it is that men are tried by false doctrine, and even by the immoralities of professing Christians.

The visible kingdom of Christ is a floor, containing a mixture of wheat and chaff; and every false doctrine is a wind which he, whose fan is in his hand, makes use of to purge it.[57] There is a great number of characters who profess to receive the truth on whom, notwithstanding, it never sat easily. Its

---

[54] Psalm 139:14.
[55] *Cavil* meaning a petty or unnecessary objection.
[56] Matthew 27:42.
[57] Ephesians 4:14.

holy and humbling nature galls their spirits. In such cases the mind is prepared to receive any representation of the gospel, however fallacious, that may comport with its desires. Being thus averse to the truth, God frequently, in just judgment, suffers the winds of false doctrine to sweep them away. Such is the account prophetically given of the chief instruments in the Romish apostasy. The introduction of that mystery of iniquity is thus described:

> Whose coming is after the working of Satan, with all power, and signs, and lying wonders, and with all deceivableness of unrighteousness, in them that perish; because they received not the love of the truth, that they might be saved. And for this cause God shall send them strong delusions that they should believe a lie that they all might be damned who believed not the truth, but had pleasure in unrighteousness (2 Thess. 2:9–12).

Not only is false doctrine permitted, that it may sweep away hypocritical characters; but the discordance, which appears amongst the professors of Christianity, is itself a temptation to many, and that in diverse ways. Some who consider themselves as almost, if not altogether, infallible, are hereby furnished with a plea for intolerance and persecution. In this way it operated much in former ages, and a portion of it is still prevalent amongst us. "You see," say they, "whither this liberty of conscience will lead men. If they be left to themselves to form their own notions of religion, there will be no end to their errors and divisions and to the sects that will rise out of them." Thus the Catholics attempted to discredit congregational church government as fruitful of sects and divisions.

But if either of them were required to prove that there is less error or opposition amongst themselves than amongst their neighbours, they might find it a difficult task. On one side, men find it necessary either not to think at all, or to conceal their sentiments; on the other, they speak and write their minds with greater freedom—but things are what they are, whether they be avowed or not. He who persecutes men for their errors may at last be found equally erroneous himself; but allowing that he is not, and that his creed is orthodox, yet is he far from being sound in the faith in the scriptural sense of the words? He "knows not what manner of spirit he is of."[58] He may be willing to fight, but has yet to learn what are those weapons by which the soldiers of the Lamb are enabled to overcome.

Others, on the same ground, have rejected all religion. "You cannot agree," say they, "as to what is truth: settle it among yourselves before you attempt to trouble us with it." Very well. If you can satisfy your consciences with this evasion, do so. It will not avail you at death or judgment. You will then be reminded that you did not reason thus in things to which your hearts were inclined; but applied with all your powers, and used every possible means to ascertain the truth

[58] Luke 9:55.

for yourselves, and acted accordingly. On your own principles, therefore, will you be judged.

Others, who have not gone these lengths, have yet been tempted to despair of finding out what is the true religion. "Amidst the opposition of opinion which continually presents itself before us, say they, how are we, plain people, to judge and act?" If you mean to intimate that it is vain for you to concern yourselves about it, that is the same as saying, "it is vain to attempt anything that is accompanied with difficulties," or to walk in any way that is attended with temptations. This thinking would lead you to stand still in other things as well as in religion. But if it be the real desire of your soul to know the right way, and walk in it, there is no reason to despair.

Follow no man as your guide, but go to your Bible and your God, and there decide the question. You need not say in your heart, "Who shall ascend into heaven; or who shall descend into the deep? The word is near you."[59] To read controversial books may, in many cases, be useful, but seldom when it is done with a view to decide the great question: what is the right way to everlasting life? A book as well as a sermon may be the means of affording such direction. But when the mind is in a state of suspense, it is beyond all comparison, the safest to consult the oracles of God. To launch into controversy without having obtained satisfaction on the first principle of the doctrine of Christ is to put to sea in a storm

[59] Romans 10:6–9.

without a rudder. One great reason why men are carried about with diverse and strange doctrines is that their "hearts are not established with grace."[60] They have no principles of their own and, therefore, are carried away with anything that wears the appearance of plausibility.

But one of the worst inferences that is drawn from the discordant doctrines which abound in the world is that doctrine itself is of little or no account. As intolerance and bigotry, under the specious name of zeal, distinguished former ages; so skeptical indifference, under the specious names of candour, liberality, and moderation, distinguishes this. This is the grand temptation, perhaps, of the present times. It would seem as if men must either fight for truth with carnal weapons, or make peace with error. Either our religious principles must be cognizable by human legislators, or they are neither good nor evil, and God himself must not call us to account for them. Either we must call men masters upon earth, or deny that we have any master even in heaven.

It is a favourite principle with unbelievers and with many professing Christians who verge towards them, that error not only has its seat in the mind, but that it is purely intellectual, and therefore innocent. Hence they plead against all church censures, and every degree of unfavorable opinion, on account of doctrinal sentiments, as though it were a species of persecution. But if the causes of error be principally moral, it

---

[60] Hebrews 13:9.

will follow that such conclusions are as contrary to reason as they are to Scripture.

The above remarks are far from being designed to cherish a spirit of bitterness against one another, as men, or as Christians. There is a way of viewing the corruption and depravity of mankind so as to excite bitterness, wrath, and every species of evil temper. There is also a way of viewing them that, without approving or conniving at what is wrong, shall excite the tear of compassion. It does not become us to declaim against the wickedness of the wicked in a manner as if we expected grapes of thorns, or figs of thistles but while we prove ourselves the decided friends of God, to bear good-will to men. It becomes those who may be the most firmly established in the truth as it is in Jesus to consider that a portion of the errors of the age, in all probability, attaches to them. Even though it were otherwise, yet they are directed to carry it benevolently towards others who may err:

In meekness instructing those that oppose themselves; if God, peradventure, will give them repentance, to the acknowledging of the truth (2 Tim. 2:25).

Finally, there is an important difference between raising the foundation, and building upon them with portions of wood, hay, and stubble. It becomes us not to make light of either—but the latter may be an object of forbearance, whereas the former is not. With the enemies of Christ, we ought, in religious matters, to make no terms. Towards his friends, though in some respects erroneous, it behooves us to come as near as it is possible to do without a dereliction of principle. A truly Christian spirit will feel the force of such language as the following, and will act upon it:

> All that in every place call upon the name of Jesus Christ our Lord, both theirs and ours, grace be to them, and peace from God our Father, and from the Lord Jesus Christ—Grace be with all them that love our Lord Jesus Christ in sincerity! (1 Cor. 1:2–3; Eph. 6:24).

Scripture Index

Psalms

27:8b	13
139:14	35

Jeremiah

13:16	22

Matthew

18:11	4
21:25–26	28
26:28	8
27:3	20
27:42	36

Luke

9:55	38

John

3:16	4
8:32	13
8:43	4
14:6	4
17:17	13

Acts

4:12	6
10:43	5
16:30	10

Romans

2:6	10
6:14	11
6:17	12
10:6–9	39
10:9	7
13:13	15
14:16	31
14:17–20	2

1 Corinthians

1:2–3	42
1:23	5
2:2	5
2:6–7	33
2:12	28, 33
2:14	27
2:15–16	33
3:1–2	32, 33
3:12–17	33
11:19	35
13:7	19
15:1–4	5
15:33	15

2 Corinthians

5:10	10
5:16	18
11:4	12

Galatians

3:1	16
4:11	16
4:19	16
4:20	16
5:7	16
5:17	16
5:26	16

Ephesians

1:13	11
2:2	15
4:14	36
4:32	15
6:24	42

Philippians

3:14	13

Colossians

1:23	11

2 Thessalonians

2:9–12	37
2:10	20

1 Timothy

1:11	14
1:15	5
4:1	26

2 Timothy

2:17	10
2:25	41
3:1–2	26
3:5	29
3:8	29
3:7	26
3:14	11
4:3–4	32

Hebrews

3:7–13	17
12:15–16	17
13:9	39

James

1:18	13
2:18	10

1 Peter

2:1	6

2 Peter

2:1	26
2:2	31
2:18	31

1 John

2:23	8
4:1–6	12
5:1	7
5:5	7
5:11	6, 8
5:12	8

2 John

1:1–13	19
1:2	18
1:9–11	19

3 John

1:1	18
1:4	3, 14

FURTHER READING ON ANDREW FULLER

Paul Brewster, *Andrew Fuller: Model Pastor-Theologian* (Studies in Baptist Life and Thought; Nashville, TN: B&H, 2010).

Andrew Gunton Fuller, *Andrew Fuller* (London: Hodder & Stoughton, 1882).

Keith S. Grant, *Andrew Fuller and the Evangelical Renewal of Pastoral Theology* (Studies in Baptist History and Thought, vol. 36; Milton Keynes, England: Paternoster, 2013).

Michael A.G. Haykin, *One heart and one soul: John Sutcliff of Olney, his friends, and his times* (Darlington, Co. Durham: Evangelical Press, 1994).

Michael A.G. Haykin, ed. *'At the Pure Fountain of Thy Word': Andrew Fuller as an Apologist* (Studies in Baptist History and Thought, vol. 6; Carlisle, Cumbria, UK/Waynesboro, GA: Paternoster Press, 2004).

Gilbert Laws, *Andrew Fuller, Pastor, Theologian, Ropeholder* (London: Carey Press, 1942).

Peter Morden, *Offering Christ to the World: Andrew Fuller (1754–1815) and the Revival of Eighteenth Century Particular Baptist Life* (Studies in Baptist History and Thought, vol. 8; Carlisle: Paternoster Press, 2003).

ISBN: 978-1-77526-334-0

Fuller deals with the issue of backsliding: when genuine Christians lose their passion for Christ and his kingdom. This was not a theoretical issue for Fuller, therefore, and his words, weighty when he first wrote them, are still worthy of being pondered—and acted upon.

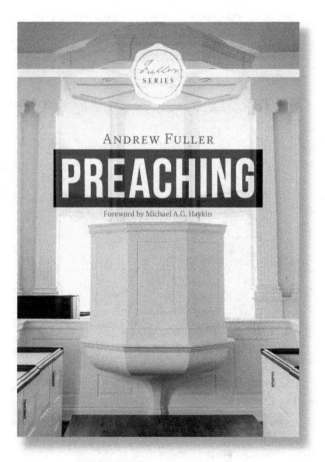

Fuller wrote to encourage a young minister in sermon preparation and reading this work will be of great value to any preacher today.

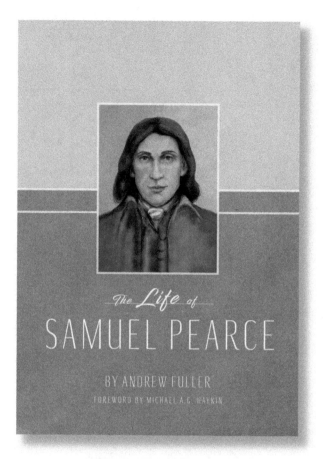

ISBN: 978-1-77526-339-5

In the eyes of Fuller, Samuel Pearce (1766–1799) was the epitome of the spirituality of their community. In fact, in that far-off day of the late eighteenth century Pearce was indeed well known for the anointing that attended his preaching and for the depth of his spirituality. It was said of him that "his ardour … gave him a kind of ubiquity; as a man and a preacher, he was known, he was felt everywhere."

Date Completed	Name

H&E *Publishing*

WWW.HESEDANDEMET.COM

IN PARTNERSHIP WITH

Andrew Fuller

CENTER *for* BAPTIST STUDIES
at THE SOUTHERN BAPTIST THEOLOGICAL SEMINARY

www.andrewfullercenter.org

OTHER PUBLICATIONS BY H&E

John Bunyan, *Saved By Grace*

Samuel Pearce, *Selected Works*

J.C. Ryle, *Baxter*

J.C. Ryle, *Latimer*

J.C. Ryle, *Whitefield*

ABOUT

H&E Publishing

H&E Publishing is a Canadian evangelical publishing company located out of Peterborough, Ontario. We exist to provide Christ-exalting, Gospel-centred, and Bible-saturated content aimed to show God to be as glorious and worthy as He truly is.

We seek to provide rich resources that will equip, nourish, and refresh the Christian's soul. We desire to make available a variety of works that serve this purpose in the church. One key area of focus is to revive evangelicals of the past through updated reprints.

ABOUT

Andrew Fuller

CENTER for BAPTIST STUDIES

at THE SOUTHERN BAPTIST THEOLOGICAL SEMINARY

The Andrew Fuller Center for Baptist Studies, located at The Southern Baptist Theological Seminary in Louisville, Kentucky, seeks to promote the study of Baptist history as well as theological reflection on the contemporary significance of that history. The center is named in honor of Andrew Fuller (1754–1815), the late eighteenth- and early nineteenth- century English Baptist pastor and theologian, who played a key role in opposing aberrant thought in his day as well as being instrumental in the founding and early years of the Baptist Missionary Society.

Notes:

Notes:

Notes:

Notes:

Notes:

Notes:

Notes:

Notes:

Notes:

Notes: